VIRUS VS. BACTERIA

KNOWING THE DIFFERENCE

BIOLOGY 6TH GRADE

Children's Biology Books

BABY PROFESSOR
EDUCATION KIDS

Speedy Publishing LLC
40 E. Main St. #1156
Newark, DE 19711
www.speedypublishing.com

Have you ever wondered what the difference is between a virus and bacteria? They are actually very different and in this book, we will be learning about what these differences are.

VIRUS

Virus Cell

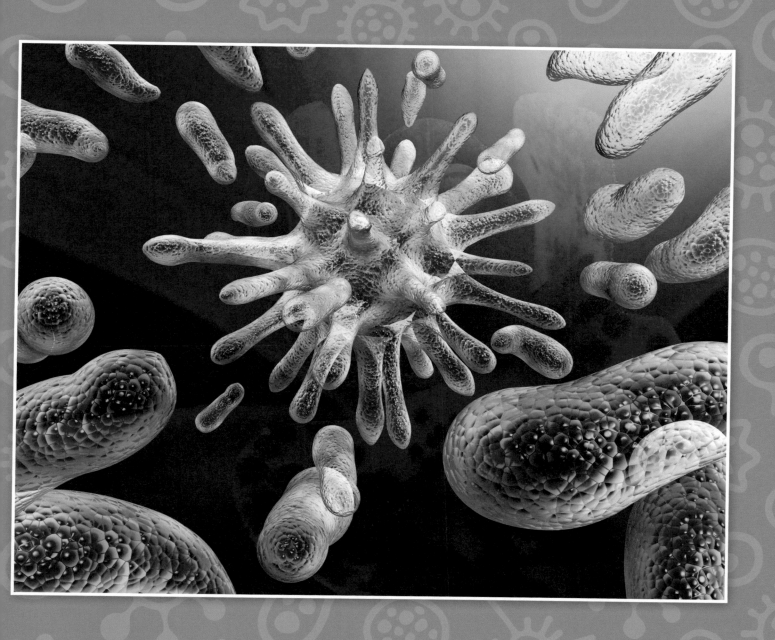

Portrait of Walter Reed

The term *"virus"* comes from the Latin term *"Virulentus"* which means *"Poisonous"*. Walter Reed discovered the first human virus in 1901, which was the yellow fever virus.

Tiny particles that can infect plants and animals and make them ill are known as viruses. They consist of genetic materials such as DNA and have a protein coating for protection.

Viruses have the ability to hijack cells of living organism by injecting genetic material directly into the cell and taking over. They are then able to use this cell for making additional viruses and taking over additional cells.

Set of handdrawn virus cells.

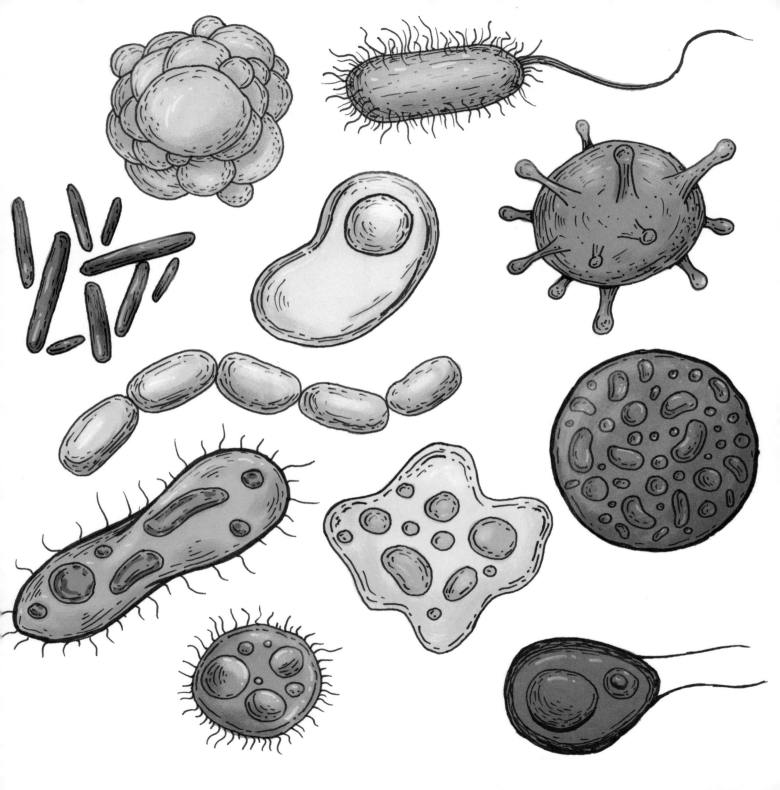

ARE THEY ALIVE?

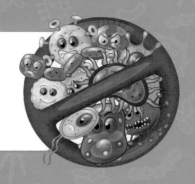

The opinions of scientists differ as to whether viruses are alive or not. Some people believe that since they are not able to reproduce without the assistance of a host, they are non-living. In addition, they don't metabolize food to energy or have cells which are organized, which typically are characteristic of living organisms.

CHARACTERISTICS

- They have no organized cell structure.

- They do not have a cell nucleus.

- Typically, they will have one or two DNA or RNA strands.

- They are protected with a protein coating known as the CAPSID.

- They are not active when they are not inside of a living cell, however, they are active once they are inside another living cell.

Human Cell and Virus Cells

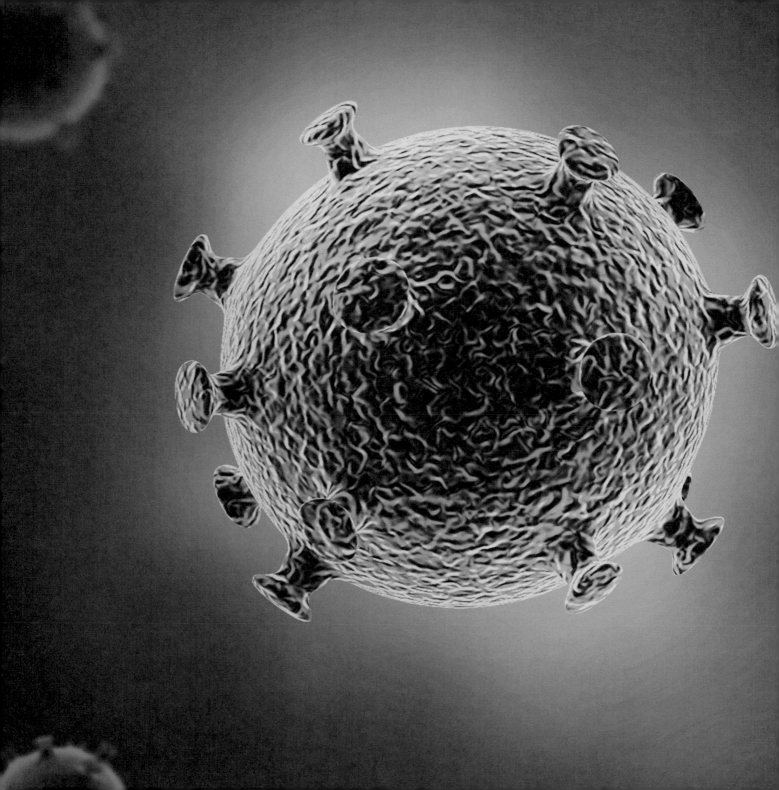

WHY ARE THEY CONSIDERED tO BE BAD?

Once they are able to invade the cell of your body and start multiplying, they make their host ill and can cause many types of diseases.

Virus Cells

HOW DO THEY SPREAD?

Viruses are lightweight and very small. They have the ability to float through the air, survive in the water, and they are even able to survive on your skin's surface. Viruses are passed from one another by shaking hands, through water, touching food, or by air once a person sneezes or coughs. In addition, they can be passed by animals, insect bites and through bad food.

Little boy coughing.

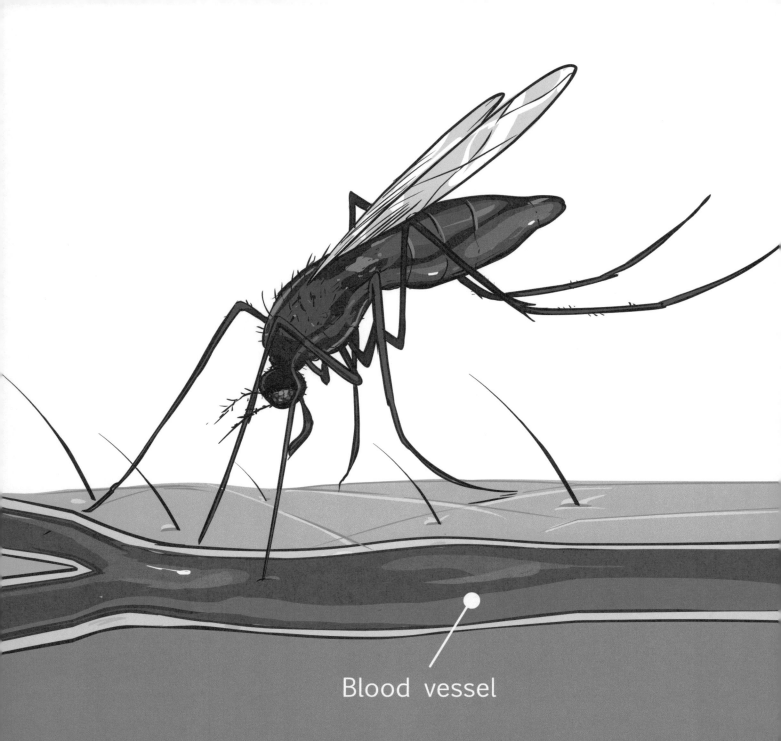

Blood vessel

TYPES OF VIRUSES

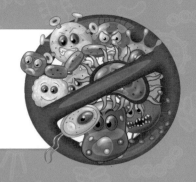

There are several viruses that have the ability to infect people and make them ill. An example of the most common is **Influenza** that can cause a person to get the flu. Some other illnesses that are caused by viruses include the common cold, mumps, yellow fever, measles and hepatitis.

Illustration of a mosquito sucking blood from human skin.

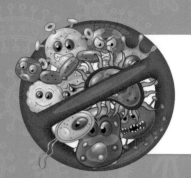

AVOIDING INFECTION

Listed here are a few things you can do to reduce your chance of getting a virus infection:

• Washing your hands, which is probably one of the most important ones.

• Keep your fingers and hands out of your eyes, nose and mouth. Rubbing your eyes or nose might move a virus that was on your hands into your body that will then infect your entire body.

Little boy rubbing his eyes.

- Be sure to cook your food until it is fully cooked, especially meat.

- Be sure to take your vitamins every day.

- Get plenty of exercise and sleep to help strengthen your immune system and fight off any virus.

Chef cooking seafood dish.

HOW ARE THEY TREATED?

Not much can be done to treat a virus. Most of time, our body's immune system will fight it off. Vaccines have been developed by scientists that assist our bodies in building up immunity to a certain virus. The flu shot is one type of a vaccine which helps our body in developing its own defense against the flu. These are known as antibodies.

Doctor vaccinates patient.

Bacteria

Bacteria Cell

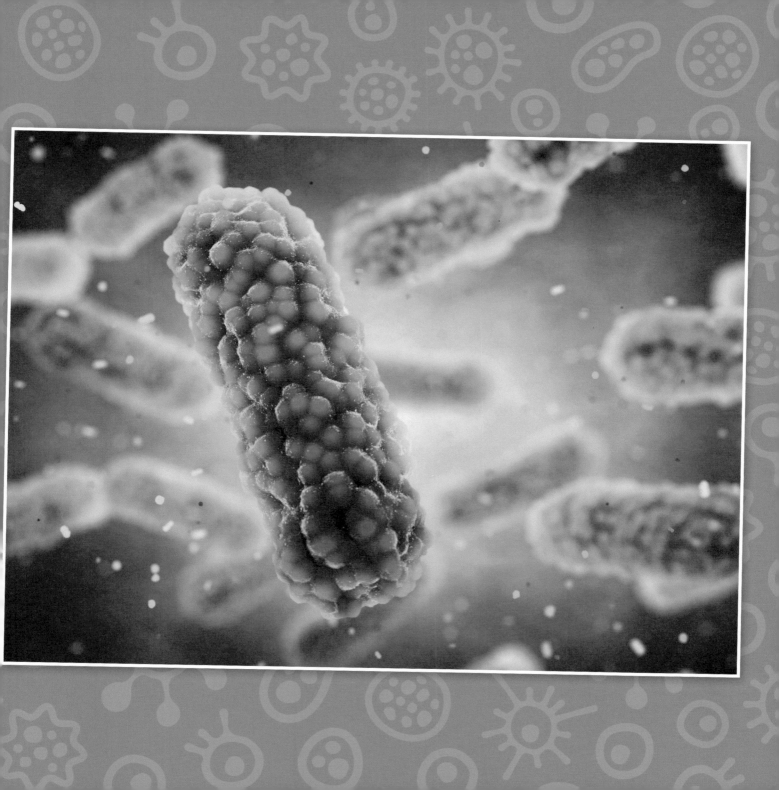

Bacteria are tiny organisms that are found everywhere surrounding us. Even though we can't see them without a microscope since they are so tiny, they can still be found on our skin, in the air, in the ground, in our bodies, and throughout all of nature.

Illustration of Dirty Hand

Bacteria are microorganisms which are single-celled and their cell structure doesn't contain a nucleus which makes them unique and most have cell walls which are similar to cells of plants. They come in many shapes that include rods, spheres, and spirals. Some can even *"swim"* around with the use of their long tails known as flagella. Others simply glide along or hang out.

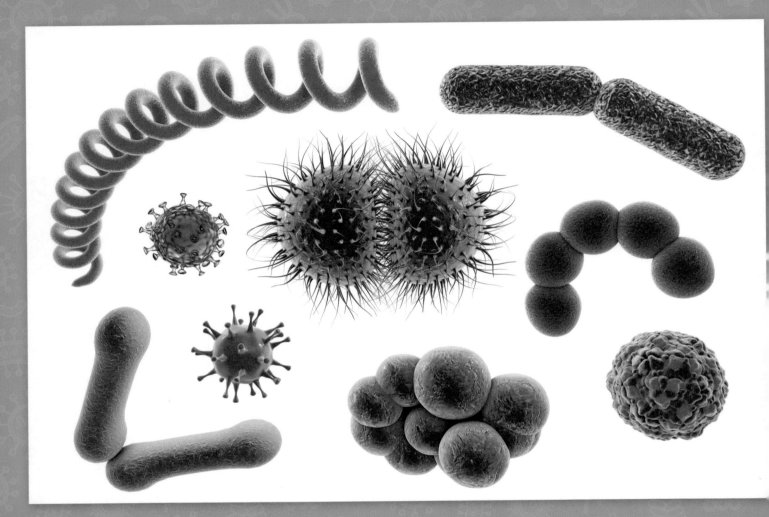

Bacteria of different shapes and viruses.

CAN BACTERIA BE DANGEROUS?

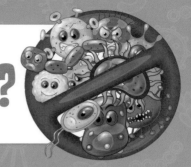

While most forms are not dangerous, some can be and can make us ill. These are known as pathogens, which can cause diseases in plants and animals. Some types of pathogens are *typhoid fever, tetanus, leprosy, pneumonia* and *food poisoning.*

ortunately, there are antibiotics we can take to help in fighting these bad pathogens. Also, there are antiseptics we can use for keeping any wounds clean of bacteria as well as antibiotic soap we can use to keep the pathogens away. Like your mom always said, *"be sure to wash your hands!"*.

Good Bacteria

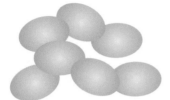
Lactococcus

Lactobacillus

Lactobacillus bifidus

Bad Bacteria

Clostridium perfringens

Staphylococcus

Escherichia coli

ARE THEY ALL BAD?

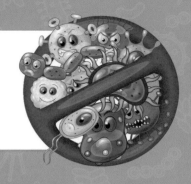

No, not at all. Most bacteria can be quite helpful to us and play a key role in the ecosystem of the planet as well as for human survival.

Bacteria in the Soil

Bacteria does a lot of work for us in the soil. One type, known as decomposers, break down the materials of dead animals and plants. While this might seem a bit gross, it is an important function and helps to get rid of the dead tissue and create soil. Rhizobium bacteria is another type that works to fertilize the soil with nitrogen that plants need to grow.

Root nodules containing Rhizobiaceae bacteria.

Sauerkraut, cucumber pickles and yogurt - popular probiotic fermented foods

BacteRia in OuR Food

Yes, there is even bacteria in our food. While you might think that is gross, they are not bad and are used to make foods such as yogurt, cheese, soy sauce and pickles.

Bacteria in Our Bodies

There are several types of good bacteria that can be found in our bodies. One of the primary uses is aiding in the digestion and breaking down of the food we eat. Some bacteria also aid our immune system by protecting us from organisms that might make us ill.

Good bacterial Flora

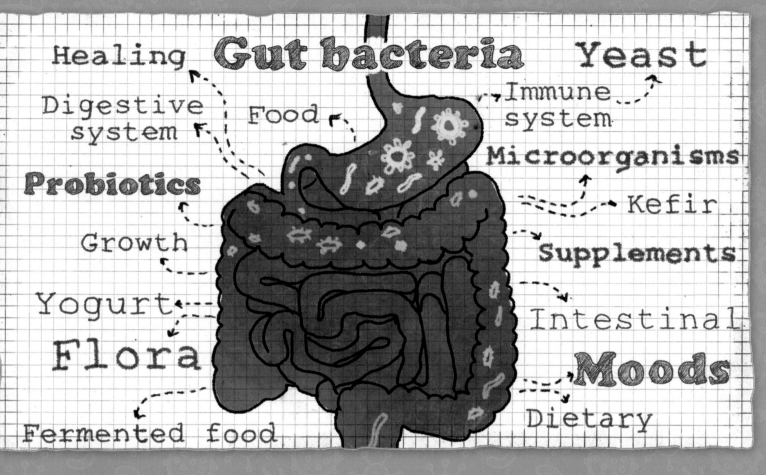

Healing **Gut bacteria** Yeast

Digestive system

Food

Immune system

Probiotics

Microorganisms

Kefir

Growth

Supplements

Yogurt

Intestinal

Flora

Moods

Fermented food

Dietary

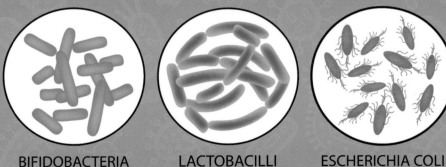

BIFIDOBACTERIA   LACTOBACILLI   ESCHERICHIA COLI

Bacteria Cell Anatomy

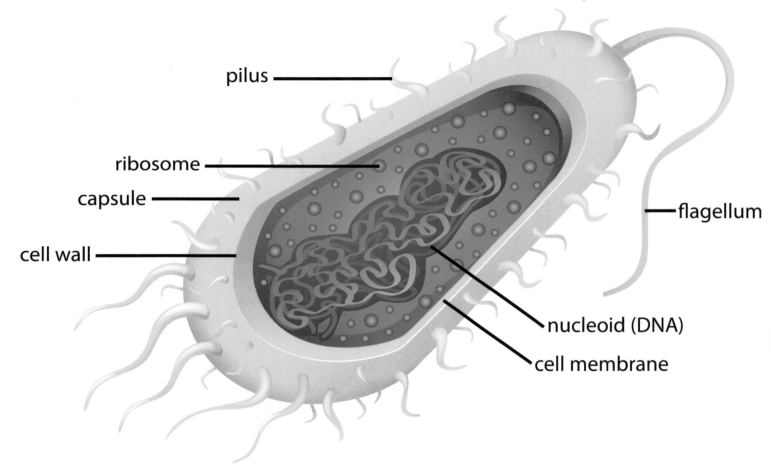

pilus

ribosome

capsule

cell wall

flagellum

nucleoid (DNA)

cell membrane

THE BACTERIA CELL

Prokaryotes is the scientific name for a bacteria cell. They are considered to be fairly simple cells since they do not contain a cell nucleus or any other specialized organelles.

FUNGi

Fungal colonies: Candida albicans

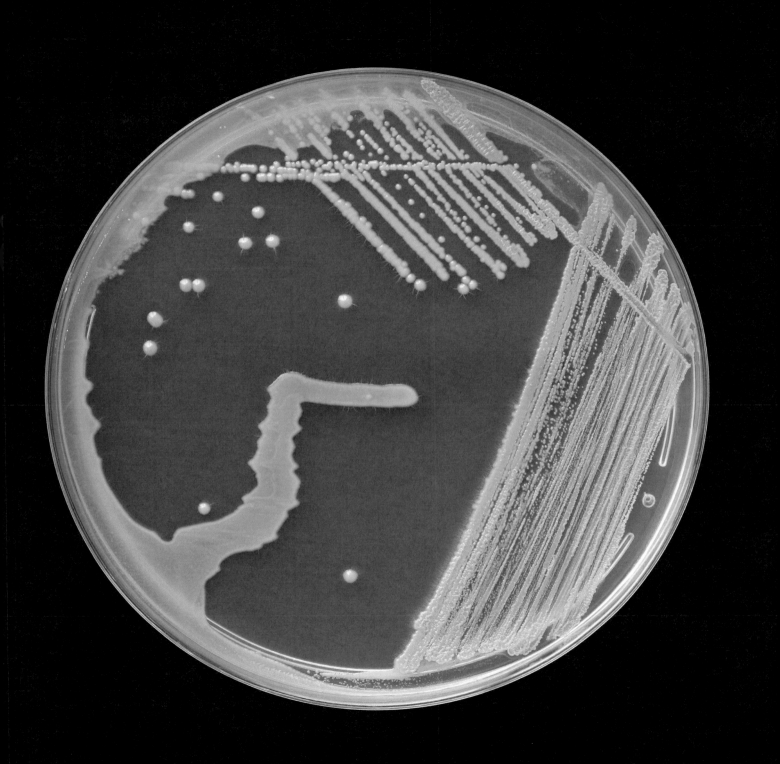

Fungi are organisms that are classified in their own kingdom which means that they are not bacteria, plants, or animals. Fungi consist of complex eukaryotic cells similar to plants and animals, unlike bacteria, which consist of simple prokaryotic cells.

Turkey tail tree fungus on a rotted fallen tree.

While it may seem strange, the fungi kingdom is more like the animal kingdom than they are to the plant kingdom. The top part of the mushroom is referred to as the cap and the small plates located underneath the cap are referred to as the gills.

They are found all over the Earth including in the Air, on Land, in Water, as well as in animals and plants. They vary greatly in their size from microscopically tiny to the biggest organisms on our planet, being many square miles big. There are over 100,000 different species that have been identified.

Fungi. Classification based on cell division.

FUNGI

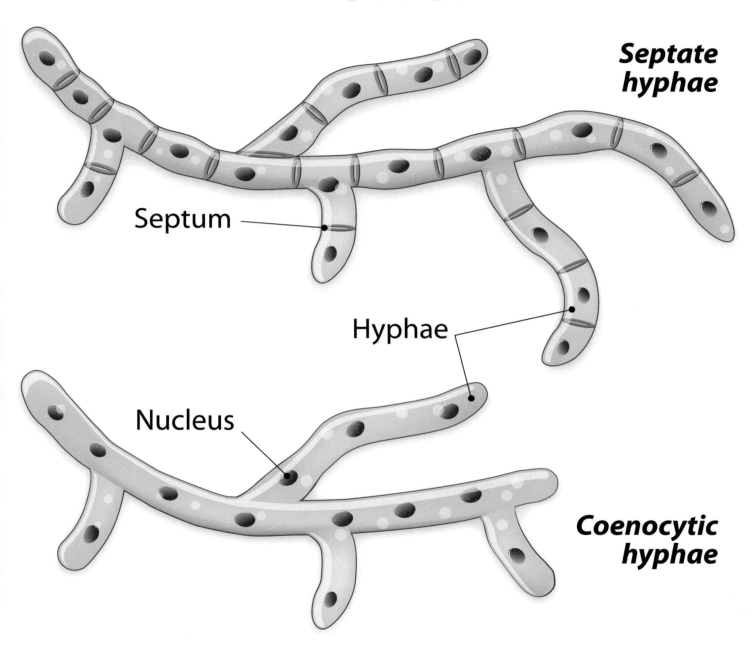

Septate hyphae

Septum

Hyphae

Nucleus

Coenocytic hyphae

HOW DO THEY DIFFER FROM PLANTS?

At one time, Fungi were classified as plants. There are two major differences, however: (1) their cell walls consist of chitin other than cellulose and (2) they don't create their own food such as plants do using photosynthesis.

CHARACTERISTICS

Some characteristics of Fungi are

• They are eukaryotic

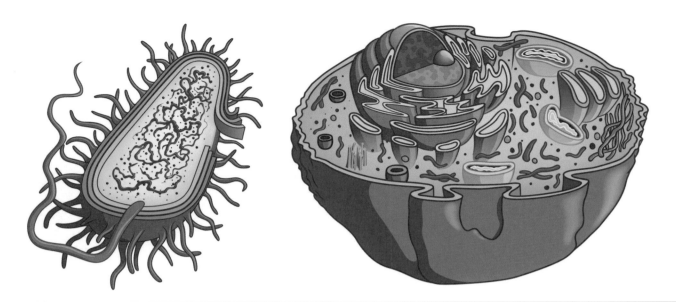

Illustration of Prokaryote and Eukaryote cell cross-section.

- They obtain their food by eating off of their hosts or by decomposing matter

- Unlike plants, they do not have chlorophyll

- They reproduce with spores rather than seeds, fruit, or pollen

- They are not able to actively move around.

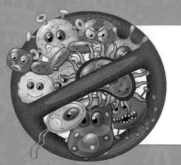

FUNGi ROLeS

FOOD - Many types of fungi such as truffles and mushrooms are used as food. A type of fungi known as yeast is used to help bread rise and also in fermenting beverages.

DECOMPOSITION - Fungi are essential for decomposition of organic matter. This is necessary for several of the cycles of life including the oxygen, nitrogen, and carbon cycles. In breaking the organic matter down, fungi release oxygen, nitrogen, and carbon into the atmosphere and soil.

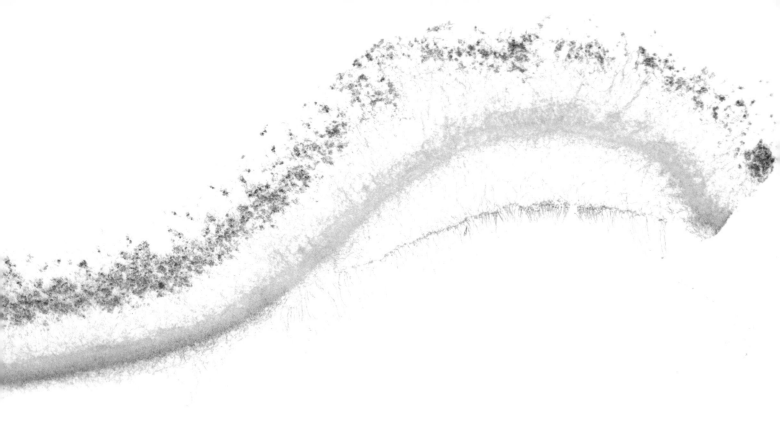

Penicillin under the microscope, (Penicillium W.M).

MEDICINE - Some are used in killing bacteria that causes disease and infections in humans. They are used in making antibiotics such as cephalosporin and penicillin.

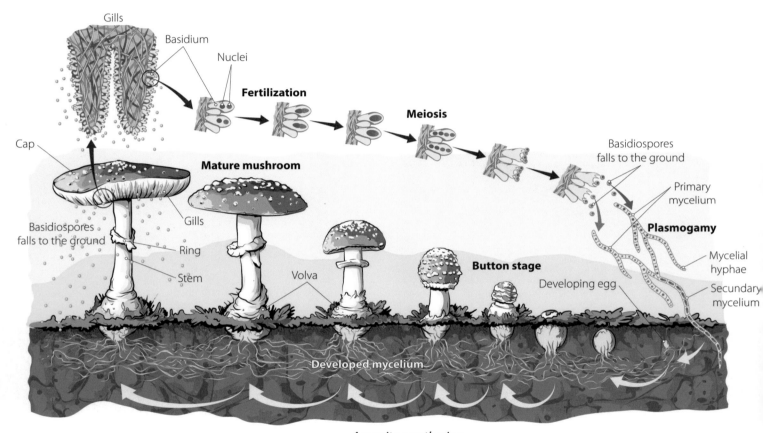

Gills

Basidium

Nuclei

Fertilization

Meiosis

Cap

Mature mushroom

Basidiospores
falls to the ground

Gills

Ring

Stem

Volva

Basidiospores
falls to the ground

Primary
mycelium

Plasmogamy

Mycelial
hyphae

Secundary
mycelium

Button stage

Developing egg

Developed mycelium

Amanita pantherina

Mushroom life cycle (Amanita Pantherina).

Different Types of Fungi

Scientists have divided fungi into four groups: *Molds, Club Fungi, Sac Fungi* and *Imperfect Fungi*. Examples of more common fungi that you might use or see in everyday life are listed next.

Mushrooms are a part of the group known as club fungi and are the fruiting part of a fungus. Some of them are used as food and good to eat, but others can be very poisonous. This is why you should never eat one that you find out in the woods!

Molds are created using filaments known as *Hyphae.* They have a tendency to form on old bread, fruit and cheese. Occasionally, the hyphae grow upward and appear furry, then releasing additional spores from their tips.

YEASTS are round tiny organisms that are single-celled. As discussed earlier, they are important in the fermenting of beer and making bread rise.

Moldy Bread

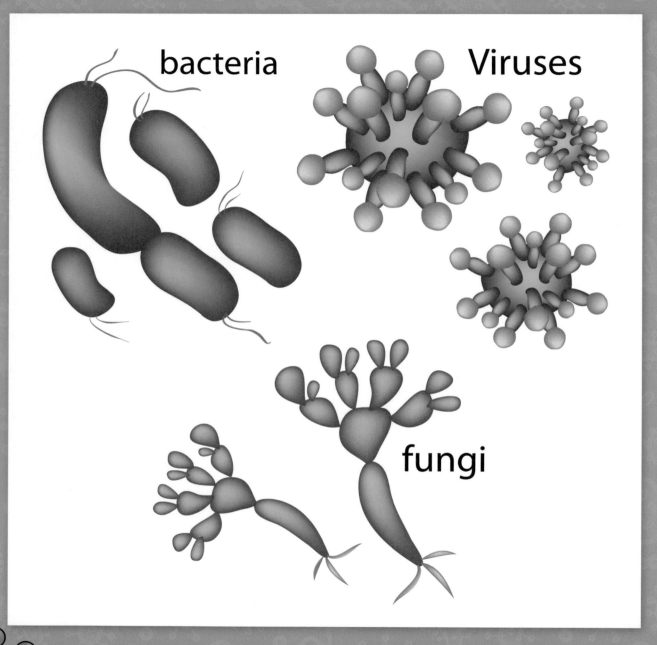

bacteria

Viruses

fungi

Now that you have learned about viruses and bacteria as well as their differences, will you be washing your hands more? The next time you see a piece of cheese or bread with *"green"* on it, what will you do with it? These are all great things to know to keep yourself healthy as well as those around you.

Visit

BABY PROFESSOR
EDUCATION KIDS

www.BabyProfessorBooks.com

to download Free Baby Professor eBooks
and view our catalog of new and exciting
Children's Books

Made in United States
Troutdale, OR
12/02/2023